The pieces that make Me, Me

Alba Moreno Russell

BookLeaf Publishing

Presentation by *BookLeaf Publishing*

Web: www.bookleafpub.com

E-mail: info@bookleafpub.com

ISBN: 978-93-95890-41-0

First edition 2022

DEDICATION

To my Big sister, my Biggest ally. A star in my sky. May she rest in forever peace. I miss you every day...that is all

To my mom, I know you did the best to your ability. No one knows better than us how much you went through as well. I appreciate how hard you tried.

To my In-Laws, for opening your arms and taking me in as one of you. For loving me and not treating any of us differently than your own. You will never understand the impact it continues to have.

This is for you.

ACKNOWLEDGEMENT

I have to start by thanking my children; Brandyn, Tehya and Julian. You three drive me crazy but also drive me to be my best. Te amo Mas que Mi propia Vida, Hasta el Final!

To my hubby, the Alpha to my Alpha, my hurricane and my calm, Markus. You are the reason I will not fail. Your confidence in me and encouragement by my side keeps me from faltering. I am forever yours and you are mine. My Beast in this life until the next.

To my brother and late sister; Alberto and Dania. I love you for your constant loyalty and unwavering support throughout our life. To my baby brother, Donni. I love you and know, that I will always believe you could do greatness.

Lastly I want to thank everyone else who has ever crossed my path. You taught me that everyone enhances your life either by being a lesson or an experience.

Each important to my personal growth.

You have taught me that life is constant movement. At times it is calm and easy and at others, the world goes upside down and you fight to catch your bearings. Both equally important.

I can only hope I have had a impact on some in return, no matter how small it may be.

PREFACE

Welcome to the world of me!

Sharing my story in a creative way aids me on my journey mentally, spiritually and emotionally. A constant reminder of where I have been, to where I have fought to be.

I hope life has treated you kindly and if not, know you are not alone.

Remember every day is a new day to kick a** and do differently. Different from your childhood, different from your yesterday and different from today. Nothing is permanent.

Human Need

Not everyone experiences
the silence
darkness
and solitude;
The birthdays remembered
life celebrated
feelings of inclusion never questioned.
But sometimes,
there are those
in the shadows
pining
longing to belong
Fighting against the invisible hands
holding them under the surface.
Sometimes,
a small flicker of light remains
protected by walls to keep from extinguishing.
Not everyone experiences
rainbows
unicorns
and sugarplums
But all
hope
crave
seek

to be seen
to be loved
to be accepted.

Universal Sadness

The clouds looming, like a blanket across the
sky,
a wolf howling to the moon.
Forgotten tears falling from my eyes,
the day is ending soon.

A wolf howling to the moon,
singing in pain from the loss.
The day is ending soon,
trees succumb to moss.

Singing in pain from the loss,
petals closing for the night.
Trees succumb to moss,
losing the will to fight.

Petals closing for the night,
bidding farewell to the stars.
Losing the will to fight,
lost in the battle of scars.

Bidding farewell to the stars.
forgotten tears falling from my eyes.
Lost in the battle of scars,
the clouds looming, like a blanket across the sky.

This is Us

Broken glass and loud music.
Clouds of smoke permeated the air.
No where to go, nowhere to hide,
memories of a child's lair.

Comforting hands and tight embraces,
eludes this darkening space.
Strangers crashing, Neighbors yelling, Teens
laughing.
Blood smeared across their face.

Historical warzone and missing persons,
childhood dreams pass us by.
Forever seeking solitude, love and trust.
Never granted wishes made upon the sky

Phoenix Mother

17 years old and counting down the days of
meeting my first son.
The one who will quickly change my ways to a
life I felt I won.
Never did I expect this bundle to bring out the
light within.
Of a heart that was once so cold now completely
softened.

20 Years old, it's time again to meet my greatest
fear.
A mother/daughter relationship to attain, an
insecurity appears.
Never did I imagine this deep relief upon
meeting this chubby girl.
Knowing without a doubt, I'd protect her against
this world.

28 years old, much has changed, we welcome
another boy.
A final piece we had gained that brought us so
much joy.
A little brother to two great siblings; pride in
what we've created.

Goodbye to shadows, hello to beginnings.
The Phoenix mother has risen.

Burning Bright

Will this fire inside elude his eyes?
Beyond the night of complete solitude
Gripping him tightly, a cause of surprise
Collapsing the inner mind, once seclude

Working through the hurricane and impulse
Hearing the voice to transcend and transform
Unlearning the skewed, personal appulse
Accepting the soft arms, wrapped within warmth

At times the road seems completely unclear
Unique and unknown to the life deserved
Ragged and tired, the end drawing near
Clawing through the light, what do we preserve?

Love, Light and Growth were about to
commence
This journey through the embers was intense.

Dear Sister

I want to write my words to you,
the ones I never spoke.
You left this world unexpectedly,
that's when my heart just broke.

The years I wasted distanced from you,
the times I left you aside.
Your heart wasn't supposed to stop beating,
I needed and wanted more time.

I didn't have enough days with you,
trying to make up for the past.
Through the years you rescued & protected me,
and I hate that I couldn't save you back.

I love you more than words can express,
and miss you every minute of the day.
It's not getting any easier,
I still had so much to say.

It's hard to face the world each day,
knowing you're not here.
No more birthdays, inside jokes or nightly calls,
These memories make it hard to bare.

This pain I feel from losing you,
it crashes over me in waves.
I want you here beside me,
but I couldn't make you stay.

I hope you knew how much I loved you;
My sister, My soul mate, My confidant.
I hope you felt how much you meant,
That's all I really want....

Listen to the Universe

The night sky soothes us
Our mind, Our body, Our soul
Answers amongst stars

Secrets of Within

Between you and I
I fear the unknown.
Between you and I
I have no where to go.

Between you and her
Smiles hide the pain.
Between you and her
Her demons never slain.

Between you and him
Hardworking tears not shown
Between you and him
Animosity has grown

Between you and them
A lavish life is seen
Between you and them
There's darkness behind a screen

Ode to my kidlets

Without you there is no me.
My breath of fresh air, my hurricane and calm.
You are the teachers of my soul,
universal work of art,
a dream never dreamed.
Reality of my growth.
Unknowingly giving strength during the darkest moments.
My very being drowning in exhaustion and grief,
yet waking to smiles and hugs,
small victories that keep me going.
There's days when it feels too much,
the dinners, the schedules, the non stop crazy,
I drag my feet to get through the day;
I won't pretend its easy.
Then I hear "I love you" while your little arms wrap tight,
every tear I shed, yawn I suppress
feels like a distant memory.
I see you laying there, sleeping snug while the day drifts away,
unaware of generational curses breaking, a new future is underway.

I give thanks to the universe for choosing me as your mother,
for the tired arms, sleepless nights, spills and all the tantrums.
Because without you there is no me.

Once upon a time...

I have traveled the world, seen many things,
met ghosts, monsters and hero's.
I have sat with the Queen, fought with Athena
listening to Hamlet dozing on a pillow.

I attended Gatsby's party, caused mischief with
the Cat,
had a burger with Pony and moped with Eeyore.
I have taken down empires, listened to Allie,
solved mysteries and witnessed the cold war .

I have built relationships, lost loved ones,
felt their anger, happiness and fears.
Cried at goodbyes, lost in these nights,
shedding more than my share of tears.

Solid spines, beautiful worlds,
exploring and adventure never ending.
Chapter after Chapter, page after page,
The last one forever impending.

Surprising Love

Locked instantly
an invisible embrace,
framing those deep brown eyes.
Slowly move downwards,
our breath hitches at the curve of her neck,
smooth skin speckled with the marks of beauty.

Gazing intently at this god given temple
Colored
Marred with a past of disbelief.
Tattoos speak of unforgettable moments -
memorialized like a shrine
Fingers trace each scar,
one after another
feather touched, admiration of the spine standing
tall.

Visible pride shines through
aware of the boulders these shoulders have
carried.

Strong hands grip my body that's held life
Stripes proudly displayed; scars of a 9-month
battle
Eyes slide downward once more to gaze upon

Those prickled Legs
That Ass
Two pillars hold a goddess strong

Eyes connect once more,
A tear slides down her cheek
The depth of love pushes through with an exhale
A smirk of respect.

Warm arms wrap around her,
she is cherished and supported.
My own eyes staring back.
Embracing

My Womanhood.
My Power.

If I was a Ghost

If I was a ghost
I'd walk close by and listen to the whispers
around me
If I was a ghost
I'd attend family occasions and sit where they
would not see
If I was a ghost
I'd watch the smiles and laughter from afar
If I was a ghost
I'd lay every night under the stars

But....
I am human
I walk close by and listen to the whispers around
me
I am a human
I attend family occasions and am not seen
I am a human
I watch the smiles and laughter from afar
I am a human
I lay alone each night under the stars

Ribbon on my finger

A reminder of sorts for which I am thankful.
The things meant to break me, gave me strength to push harder.
I am thankful for days I sought comfort and received echoed cry's in return.
For it taught me to sooth my soul in nature, a source of constant warmth.
With every bruise and harsh word, I am thankful.
For it gave me the confidence to spread kindness.
For every heartache meant to crush me, I am thankful, it has taught me to love deeper.
For it all, I am thankful.

I am thankful for the absentees, for the motivation to seek solace, bringing beauty into my world and a beast alongside it.
For this beast I am thankful.
Through tears and sweat, I found myself and my spirit.
The flowers that surround me, the water that flows, sun in the sky, moon of the night I am thankful.

Reminders of relief found in existence.
I am thankful for it all, for it brought me to me.

To my Children

If ever comes a day where you can not come to
me
Remember my words clearly.

Trust your instincts, they'll rarely steer you
wrong.
Say please and be thankful of those that give you
a piece of them,
cherish those bits of others radiant souls
its rare and a sight to be seen.

Shake another hand firmly.
Sit: listen to the elders.
Their stories are a world you could never
imagine.

Take advice, learn from others but lead your
own journey.
Treat all with respect even if they do not know
the meaning.
That's not to say be a doormat
but
control how you react.
Their actions tell
A lot.

Never give them satisfaction to take you out of your character.

Protect each other Fiercely,
Life will happen but you're never alone with each other.
Be humble always
give when you can.
You can not dictate what others do, only yourself,
So be kind.
Treat people as a blessing,
Unless they prove to be a curse.
Some will sting you; most will not.
Remain soft in this harsh world,
there is no comfort in a rock.

Remember nothing is forever,
The good
The bad
The in-between
Every day can bring something new.
Enjoy the little things, at one time they were your biggest things.
Splash in puddles, roll down a hill
Sing in the shower, feel the breeze and still.

You were meant for greatness.
My eldest, never lose your wit

My middle, keep standing tall
My youngest, always see the best

If ever comes a day where you can not find me
If I am not here
remember
no matter how far I go, I am forever near.

Until she met a boy

She never knew what love was
She dared not even seek it
A heart giving, never waiting to receive

She never knew what trust was,
She dared never to believe
A truthful voice, never waiting to hear

She never knew what warmth was,
She dared never to stoke the fire
A welcomed embrace, never waiting limbs

All she gave, never returned
Never asking, left undisturbed.
She didn't know life was blurred
Years left to unlearn.

Until she met a boy

She opened her heart, she knows she deserves
She demanded honesty, listens to the actions
She cherished the clutches, inhales the seconds

All she gave, given in return
Never asking, old ways burned.

She didn't know life was blurred
He helped her unlearn the learned.

The little things

Inspiring it is
Blue strokes
Floating in the river
Lilies dancing on the surface
The chirp of a bird
Fluttering through the sky.
Inspiration inside
Eyes of a child
Twirling around
Arms spread wide
Giggles felt
Vibrating the earth.
Inspired by
The winds embrace
A leaf's hello
The crunch underneath
The moons goodnight.

Another day

Sit for a moment
Lose yourself amongst the noise
The sun will rise again

The start of the beginning

The decision was not clear,
just there in my reach
yet never really near.
Minutes, days, weeks flew by
forever sitting on uncertainty
Do I or don't I?

What comes from indecisiveness
but more indecisiveness.
Voices heard bickering in the background
of the mind.
Seeking advice from
another who is sound.

Taking the jump,
filled with fear and anxiety,
a need to get over the slump.
Make a difference in society,
a change from the norm.
The motivation behind it all?
Build a home that is cozy and warm.

www.ingramcontent.com/pod-product-compliance
Lightning Source LLC
Chambersburg PA
CBHW051753130826
49812CB00033B/1127
9789395890410